$180°C = \sim 350° - 375°F$

BBQ

200 TASTY RECIPES

igloo

Published in 2009
by Igloo Books Ltd
Cottage Farm
Sywell
NN6 0BJ
www.igloo-books.com

10 9 8 7 6 5 4 3 2 1

ISBN: 978 1 84817 485 6

Project Managed by R&R Publications Marketing Pty Ltd

Publisher: Anthony Carroll
Cover Designer: Elain Wei Voon Loh
Layout Designer: Elain Wei Voon Loh
Food Photography: Brent Parker Jones, R&R Photostudio (www.rrphotostudio.com.au)
Food Stylists: Lee Blaylock, Emma Rosen, Michelle Finn, Sebastian Sedlak
Recipe Development: Michelle Finn, R&R Test Kitchen
Proofreader: Stephen Jones

Printed and manufactured in China

Contents

Introduction

What is it about the barbecue that people love so much? Is it the wonderful smoky flavour imparted to the food? Is it the unmistakable brand of the grill bars on the food? Is it the communal style of cooking where the cook is more often the centre of attention, rather than cloistered in the kitchen?
It is all of these things and more.

Originating in the Caribbean as a "sacred fire pit" for cooking whole animals, the barbecue has worked its way into the world's culinary imagination, becoming a cherished and highly evolved method of cooking. All over the world, from Brazil to Australia, South Africa to Japan, the barbecue is an integral part of many peoples' cuisines.

The key attraction is often the timeless act of making and cooking over a fire – to some, cooking on a gas barbecue just doesn't seem right. How can food cooked over gas even begin to taste as good as that cooked over a wood or charcoal fire? This may seem to be a legitimate objection, but it is primarily emotional and romantic. The truth of the matter is that exceptional food can be produced on either a gas or charcoal barbecue, and a number of different styles of barbecue and grillers are available on today's market. No matter what your choice of barbeque or grilling style, the recipes in this book will give you exceptional results every time, regardless of which type of barbecue you use.

The first kettle shaped grills revolutionised outdoor cooking. It was the first barbecue designed to cook with the lid closed. The use of carefully designed vents in the top and bottom allow the heat to circulate, almost completely eliminating flare-ups.

The newer generation of gas grill have dials that allow you to have complete control of heat circulation, with or without a hinged hood. They are fitted with grill bars and in some cases a hotplate, for cooking those difficult ingredients that sometimes are part of a good recipe.

Equipment

The world of outdoor cooking has come a long way since the days of holding a few sausages over an open fire. Now, a few simple pieces of equipment will allow you to cook almost anything on the barbecue.

For simpler fare, little equipment is needed – in most cases standard kitchenware can be used – but be aware that barbecue cooking can take its toll on tools

not designed for this purpose. Although you do not have to purchase a great deal of equipment to enjoy barbecuing, you may find it beneficial to have some purpose-built items for your outdoor cooking.

Tongs are probably the most useful and versatile

barbecue tool that you can buy. Use a pair that is at least 12in/30cm long and spring loaded. If you are cooking over charcoal, it's not a bad idea to have two pairs – one to move the hot charcoal around and one to use with the food.

A grill brush is a must for proper grill care. It is recommended that you brush the grill before oiling and after cooking, while the grill is still hot, to remove any food particles or burned-on grease. If you follow this procedure consistently, you won't have to wash the grill with cleanser, which can ruin the seasoning.

Hinged wire baskets hold fish fillets, hamburger patties or bread between two grills secured by a latch. Simply place the food inside the basket and place over the heat. When one side is done, flip it over. You should lightly oil the basket before placing food inside.

Have all your barbecue tools ready and available before you light your fire. And always make sure you have enough charcoal or gas to cook all your food – there is nothing more frustrating than discovering that your gas has run out halfway through cooking, or that your fire is dying and there is no more charcoal.

Safety

Even though you will be cooking over a naked flame, there is no real reason to take any extra safety measures than you would when cooking indoors – common sense should still prevail. For example, make sure nobody, especially children, will be in a position to accidentally touch the hot surfaces, and never leave your barbecue unattended.

However, more care must be taken with charcoal barbecues than gas barbecues, which can be instantly turned off. Always take care when lighting your barbecue that it is not too close to buildings or overhanging branches, vines and so on. If using an accelerant to help ignite your barbecue, remember to not use too much – you're trying to light a barbecue, not a bonfire! And once your fire is lit, even if it is struggling, never try to add more accelerant – this is a recipe for disaster. It's much better to let your fire go out and start again than play around with highly flammable substances and naked flames.

When it comes to food hygiene, again there is really no need to take any extra precautions than you would when cooking in your kitchen. For example, ensure all your food is fully defrosted before you begin cooking, and make sure raw and cooked foods are kept on separate plates. However, since barbecuing is generally a summer activity, you should be wary of leaving food out of the refrigerator for too long as bacteria love those long, summer days just as much as we do!

When is the barbecue ready?

It does not take long for gas barbecues to heat up. Lightly oil your grill and hotplate, and as soon as you see the first few wisps of smoke you will know they are ready to cook on. One of the great advantages of gas barbecues is the ability to continually adjust their temperature, so make sure you make use of this feature and turn the heat up or down, depending on your requirements.

Charcoal barbecues require a little more attention. First you must build your fire – make sure you have enough fuel to leave a good bed of embers, as these are what you will cook on. Once the fire is lit, do not be tempted to cook on it immediately – the flames will be too hot and there will not be an even distribution of heat. The flames will burn lower and lower, and you can begin to cook over the hot coals just as the last few flames are burning away. At this point you should also try to distribute the coals evenly around your barbecue so the cooking temperature is roughly the same everywhere. You can now adjust how hot the food gets by raising or lowering the grill. It also helps to give the coals a stir every now and then to expose fresh fuel and ensure you don't develop any cold or hot spots.

When it comes to telling whether your food is cooked, most of the time this is at your discretion. The main thing you need to be aware of when barbecuing on the grill is that your food is directly exposed to the flame, so fatty and sugary foods will cook faster than others as the fats and sugars drip onto the flames causing them to flare up. This can char your food and make it inedible, so foods such as sausages, oily fish and chicken with the skin on should be cooked over a lower heat to avoid this. In fact, any cut of chicken, but especially drumsticks, should be cooked slowly to ensure it is cooked right the way through.

Let's cook!

Everyone loves a good barbecue, and with this book you will be able to create the best barbecues around. Full of exciting and memorable recipes in handy chapters including meat, seafood and vegetables, this book will enable you to realise the full potential of your barbecue and help you to create many wonderful meals for yourself and your friends and family.

Meat Feast

Classic Beef Burger with the Lot

1lb/500g lean minced steak

salt and freshly ground black pepper

1 small onion, finely chopped, plus 1 large onion, sliced

4 rashers bacon

4 eggs

4 burger buns, split and toasted

1 large handful fresh lettuce

2 tomatoes, sliced

4 slices pineapple

4 slices canned beetroot

4 slices cheese

4 tablespoons mayonnaise

1 Mix the minced steak, salt, pepper and chopped onion together. Divide the mixture into 4 portions and shape into plump patties.

2 Cook the patties over hot coals for 4 minutes on each side or until done to your liking. Fry the bacon, onion slices and eggs in a frying pan.

3 On the bottom half of each burger bun place a tablespoon of mayonnaise, lettuce, tomato, pineapple and beetroot. Top each with a burger patty, bacon, egg, onion, cheese and the bun top. Serve immediately with home-made tomato sauce (see page 83).

>

---- VARIATIONS ----
- You can use other types of mince in this recipe, for example, pork or lamb.

- For a surprise centre, mould each patty around 1 teaspoon of grated Cheddar cheese, crumbled blue cheese or sweet pickle.

Marinated Beef Strips

2lb/1kg rump steak, cut crosswise into
    long flat strips
1 large onion, sliced into rings
5 tablespoons olive oil
1 cup red wine
4 cloves garlic, chopped
1 tablespoon black peppercorns
½ cup fresh parsley leaves
¼ cup fresh thyme leaves
1 large cucumber, shaved into thin slices
    with a vegetable peeler

1 Arrange the steak and onion in a single layer in a
    dish. Combine the oil, wine, garlic, peppercorns,
    parsley and thyme, pour over the steak and
    mix lightly. Cover and refrigerate for 4 hours or
    preferably overnight.

2 Drain the meat and onions, reserving the
    marinade. Weave the strips onto oiled metal or
    soaked wooden skewers. Cook over hot coals
    until tender, basting occasionally with reserved
    marinade. Cook the onions separately until
    golden. Serve skewers with onions on a bed of
    shaved cucumber.

*Serve your guests some warm marinated olives
(see page 81) while you prepare this dish.*

VARIATIONS

• For a Greek-inspired dish, use lamb instead of
  beef and instead of the red wine use ½ cup of
  lemon juice and ½ cup of white wine. Serve on
  shaved cucumber with natural yoghurt.

serves 6

Classic Steak and Onion Sandwiches

6 lean rump steaks, cut into ½ in/1cm thick strips

3 onions, finely sliced

12 thick slices wholemeal or wholegrain bread

olive oil

large handful of fresh lettuce

3 tomatoes, sliced

½ cup quick tangy barbecue sauce (see page 84)

GINGER WINE MARINADE

1 cup red wine

½ cup olive oil

1 clove garlic, crushed

1in/2½cm piece fresh ginger, grated

1   To make the marinade, place the wine, oil, garlic and ginger in a bowl and mix to combine. Place the steaks in a shallow glass or ceramic dish. Pour the marinade over, then cover and marinate for 2–3 hours or overnight in the refrigerator.

2   Light the barbecue. Fry the onions until golden. Drain the steaks and lightly oil them. Cook on barbecue for 3–5 minutes each side or until cooked to your liking.

3   Lightly brush the bread slices with oil and cook on the barbecue for 1–2 minutes each side or until lightly toasted. To assemble the sandwiches, top 6 toasted bread slices with the lettuce, tomato, steak, onions, barbecue sauce and remaining bread slices.

VARIATIONS

• This marinade is also lovely with chicken – use 6 small, butterflied chicken fillets and substitute the red wine with white wine.

• For a steak sandwich with the lot, add 6 eggs and 6 rashers of bacon to the barbecue when the steaks are nearly done, and add these to the sandwiches with a few slices of canned beetroot.

Charred T-bone Steak with Chilli Herb Butter

1 tablespoon freshly ground black pepper

2 tablespoons olive oil

6 t-bone steaks, trimmed of excess fat

CHILLI HERB BUTTER

4½oz/125g butter, softened

¼ cup mixed fresh herbs, such as thyme, parsley and basil, chopped

1 fresh red chilli, finely chopped

1 teaspoon paprika

1 To make the chilli herb butter, place the butter, herbs, chilli and paprika in a bowl and beat to combine. Place the butter on a piece of cling film and form into a log shape. Refrigerate for 1 hour or until firm.

2 Light the barbecue to a high heat. Place the black pepper and oil in a bowl and mix to combine. Brush the steaks lightly with oil mixture, place on the barbecue and cook for 3–5 minutes each side or until steaks are cooked to your liking.

3 Cut the butter into 1in/2½cm-thick slices and top each steak with 1 or 2 slices. Serve immediately with classic potato and egg salad (see page 73).

Note: Any leftover butter can be stored in the freezer to use at a later date.

›

VARIATIONS

• The chilli herb butter is also delicious served with grilled lamb chops or cutlets and grilled vegetables such as eggplant, red and green peppers and zucchini.

serves 4

Veal Schnitzel Burger

4 crumbed veal schnitzels

large handful of fresh lettuce

2 tomatoes, sliced

4 tablespoons mayonnaise

4 burger buns, split and toasted

4 slices cheese

1 Cook the veal schnitzel on the barbecue until golden and cooked through.

2 Place the lettuce, tomato slices and 1 tablespoon mayonnaise on the bottom half of each burger roll. Top with the schnitzel, cheese and burger bun top. Serve immediately.

---- VARIATIONS ----
- Use chicken schnitzel instead of veal.
- Add bacon, pineapple and quick tangy barbecue sauce (see page 84).
- Top the schnitzel with home-made tomato sauce (page 83) and melted cheese to make a cheese burger.

Tandori Beef Ribs

2lb/1kg beef spare ribs, trimmed

2 tablespoons oil

MARINADE

1 cup natural low-fat yoghurt

½ in/1cm piece fresh ginger, grated

2 cloves garlic, crushed

1 tablespoon sweet chilli sauce

1 teaspoon ground cumin

1 teaspoon ground cardamom

¼ cup fresh coriander, finely chopped

few drops of red food colouring

1 tablespoon tamarind paste

1   To make the marinade, combine the yoghurt, ginger, garlic, chilli sauce, cumin, cardamom, coriander and food colouring in a bowl and mix well. Blend the tamarind paste with ½ cup water, then fold into the yoghurt mixture.

2   Rub the marinade onto the ribs. Arrange in a shallow dish, cover and set aside for at least 3 hours, preferably overnight.

3   Remove the ribs from the marinade and cook over hot coals until dark brown and crisp, turning once and basting with remaining marinade. Serve with sweet potato salad with pine nuts (see page 68).

> VARIATIONS

• This marinade also goes really well with chicken fillets, grilled, sliced and served on grilled bread topped with sliced cucumber and sliced red onion.

Barbecued Thai-Style Steaks

3 cloves garlic, chopped
1 chilli, deseeded and roughly chopped
1 large onion, quartered
1 bunch fresh coriander leaves
⅓ cup freshly squeezed lime juice
¼ cup Thai fish sauce
2 tablespoons soft light brown sugar
salt
6 large or 12 small minute steaks

1   Light the barbecue . Process the garlic, chilli and
onion briefly in a food processor. Add the coriander
leaves (with a few tender stems, if desired) and
process until finely chopped. Add the lime juice, fish
sauce and sugar, then add salt to taste and process
for 30 seconds. Transfer to a small saucepan and
heat gently.

2   Brush both sides of the steaks with the spice
mixture. Cook over hot coals for 1–2 minutes,
constantly brushing with the spice mixture. Spoon
any remaining mixture over steaks when serving.

*While you are waiting for this to cook, serve your guests
spicy barbecue beer nuts (see page 81).*

VARIATIONS

• Replace the beef with chicken, fish or vegetables,
such as sliced eggplant, peppers and zucchini.

• For a milder marinade, replace the chilli with ginger.

Barbecued Spicy Beef

2lb/1kg rump steak, cut into 1in/2½cm-thick steaks

1 cucumber, peeled and shaved with a vegetable peeler

1 fresh red chilli, sliced

CORIANDER MARINADE

¼ cup soy sauce

2 tablespoons vegetable oil

1 teaspoon ground coriander

¼ cup fresh coriander, finely chopped

1 tablespoon brown sugar

freshly ground black pepper

1   Place the steaks in a shallow glass or ceramic dish. To make the marinade, place soy sauce, oil, ground coriander, half the fresh coriander, the sugar and black pepper in a small bowl and mix to combine. Pour the marinade over meat, cover and set aside to marinate for at least 1 hour. Arrange overlapping cucumber slices on a large platter, cover and refrigerate until required.

2   Light the barbecue. Drain the steaks and reserve the marinade. Sear steaks on the barbecue for 1 minute each side. Move steaks to a cooler section of barbecue and cook for 3 minutes each side or until cooked to your liking. Place the reserved marinade in a small saucepan, bring to the boil and cook for 3–4 minutes. Thinly slice the steaks, arrange on top of cucumber, spoon over marinade and garnish with remaining coriander leaves and sliced fresh chilli.

3   Serve with grilled tomatoes with fresh oregano and basil (see page 76).

> **VARIATIONS**
> - Substitute the steak for chicken fillets, cook until cooked through, then slice and serve.
> - Peeled prawns also go well with this marinade.

Note: Traditionally the meat for this dish should be cooked rare.

serves 4

Bacon, Beef and Cheese Burger

1lb/500g lean minced steak

salt and freshly ground black pepper

1 small onion, finely chopped

8 slices cheese

8 rashers bacon

4 burger buns, split and toasted

1 Combine the minced meat, salt, pepper and onion and mix well. Divide the mixture into 8 portions and shape into plump patties. Cook over hot coals for about 4 minutes on each side or until done to your liking, then top with cheese. While the cheese melts, cook the bacon.

2 On each burger bun bottom place a patty with cheese, a rasher of bacon, a second patty with cheese and another rasher of bacon. Top with quick tangy barbecue sauce (see page 84) and the bun top and serve immediately.

> VARIATIONS

- The best burgers are pure meat, but the mixture may be stretched with breadcrumbs or a little finely grated carrot.

- Add 1 tablespoon Worcestershire sauce and ¼ cup freshly chopped mixed herbs to the patties for extra flavour.

Beef Kebabs

1lb/500g rump steak, 1in/2½cm thick

1 large clove garlic, finely chopped

salt

pinch of ground white pepper

2 tablespoons sweet soy sauce

2 tablespoons soy sauce

1 tablespoon lemon juice

2 tablespoons vegetable oil

1   Cut the rump steak into 1in/2½cm cubes. Place the garlic, salt and pepper in a deep bowl and mix in sweet soy sauce and lemon juice. Add the cubed rump and toss until evenly coated. Cover and marinate for at least 30 minutes or overnight in the refrigerator.

2   Thread the steak pieces onto skewers. Arrange on the barbecue over moderately hot coals and cook, turning and brushing occasionally with oil, for 5 minutes or until cooked but still tender. Serve with warm bean salad (see page 72).

VARIATIONS

- Add vegetables, such as 1in/2½cm diced pepper, onion or small button mushrooms and thread onto skewers, alternating with meat, for more colour and flavour.

- Serve skewers with gently heated, best ever peanut sauce (see page 83) for satay kebabs.

Barbecued Cheese and Onion Sausages

2lb/1kg thick sausages
2 onions, sliced
3½ oz/100g tasty cheddar cheese, grated

1 Light the barbecue, pierce the sausages several times with a fork, then add to the barbecue. Cook the sausages until golden brown all over, turning regularly to ensure even cooking. Cook the onions at the same time.

2 When cooked, horizontally slit each sausage almost through. Open the slit and add some of the onions, top with grated cheese and return to the barbecue. Prop up so the filling doesn't spill.

3 Cook until cheese melts, about 1 minute. Serve with foil barbecue potatoes with herb butter (see page 77).

> ❯

------ VARIATIONS ------------------------
- Use vegetarian sausages for a great vegetarian meal.
- Vary the filling by adding diced and fried bacon, and using avocado salsa (see page 82) instead of cheese.

Spicy Beef Burger

1lb/500g lean minced steak

2 carrots, coarsely grated

3oz/85g mushrooms, finely chopped

1 large onion or 3 shallots, finely chopped

1½ cups fresh wholemeal breadcrumbs

2 tablespoons tomato purée

1 medium egg, lightly beaten

1 clove garlic, crushed

2 teaspoons ground cumin

2 teaspoons ground coriander

1 teaspoon hot chilli powder

freshly ground black pepper

6 burger buns, split and toasted

1 Preheat the grill to medium. Light the barbecue. Place all the ingredients except the burger buns in a large bowl and mix together well.

2 Using your hands, shape the mixture into 6 round, flat patties. Cook on the barbecue for about 10–15 minutes, turning once, until lightly browned and cooked to your liking.

3 Serve on toasted burger buns with sweet chilli sauce (see page 82).

VARIATIONS

• This recipe can also be used to make meatballs – shape heaped teaspoonfuls of the mixture into balls and grill, turning frequently, until cooked. Serve with toothpicks and sweet chilli sauce for dipping.

• Try using chicken or pork mince instead of beef, and add ¼ cup finely chopped fresh ginger and ¼ cup chopped fresh coriander for extra flavour and zest.

Mixed Grill

1lb/500g chipolata sausages

4 small beef steaks

4 lamb cutlets

4 thick rashers bacon

4 eggs

8 slices thick bread, grilled

1 Light the barbecue and cook the sausages. When nearly done, add the steak, lamb and bacon. Cook to your liking, then fry the eggs.

2 Serve with the grilled bread, condiments of choice and bacon roasted potatoes (see page 80).

> **VARIATIONS**
> - Add fresh tomato halves and quartered field mushrooms to cook with the steak, lamb and bacon. Hot baked beans also make a nice addition.

Lamb Souvlaki

(Greek Meat Skewers)

¼ cup lemon juice

⅓ cup olive oil

3 cloves garlic, crushed

1 large brown onion, finely chopped

¼ cup fresh oregano, chopped

¼ cup fresh thyme, chopped

1 teaspoon paprika

2 teaspoons salt

1 teaspoon ground pepper

2lb/1kg boneless lamb leg, cut into 1½ in/4cm cubes

1 large white onion, sliced

fresh pitta bread rounds

TZATZIKI (GREEK SAUCE)

1 small cucumber, peeled, deseeded and finely
    chopped or grated

pinch of salt

1 cup thick natural yoghurt

1 clove garlic, finely chopped

¼ cup fresh mint, finely chopped

1 Mix together the lemon juice, oil, garlic, onion, oregano, thyme, paprika, salt and pepper. Place the lamb into a glass or stainless steel bowl and pour over lemon mixture. Mix through and allow to marinate for at least 2 hours or overnight.

2 To make the tzatziki, place the cucumber in a strainer over a bowl, sprinkle with salt and allow to drain for 1 hour. Combine the cucumber, yoghurt, garlic and mint and mix well. Chill until ready to serve.

3 When the meat has finished marinating, light the barbecue and thread the meat onto skewers. Barbecue the skewers, turning occasionally, until golden brown and cooked. Add the sliced onion to the barbecue and cook until golden. Remove the meat and onion from the barbecue and quickly heat the pitta bread until warm.

4 Hold pitta bread in one hand and meat skewer in the other, then gently pull the contents off the skewer into the bread. Top with the onions and tzatziki and serve immediately with tabbouleh salad (see page 74). Repeat with the other skewers, or allow guests to do their own.

❭

- - - VARIATIONS - - -
- Add fresh salad ingredients, such as sliced tomato and lettuce, to the souvlaki when serving.
- Substitute diced chicken thighs for the lamb.

Lamb Burger with Grilled Haloumi

1lb/500g lean minced lamb
¼ cup fresh breadcrumbs
¼ teaspoon cayenne pepper
2 tablespoons sweet fruit chutney
¼ cup fresh parsley, chopped
¼ cup fresh thyme, chopped
7oz/200g haloumi, cut into 4 slices
2 tomatoes, sliced
4 burger buns, split and toasted

YOGHURT SAUCE

¼ cup thick natural yoghurt
2 tablespoons Dijon mustard
¼ cup fresh mint, chopped
2 teaspoons lemon juice
¼ teaspoon cracked black pepper

1 To make the sauce, mix yoghurt, mustard, mint, lemon juice and pepper together until combined and refrigerate until needed.

2 Light the barbecue. Combine the lamb, breadcrumbs, cayenne, chutney, parsley and thyme in a medium bowl, then shape into 4 patties. Cook on the barbecue, turning occasionally, until cooked through. Cook haloumi slices until golden.

3 Place the tomato slices on the bottom half on each bun, top with a patty, haloumi, yoghurt sauce and top of bun. Serve with barbecue potato skins (see page 79).

···· VARIATIONS ····
• If preferred, beef can be used instead of lamb.
• For extra flavour, add ¼ cup chopped olives to the mixture and substitute the grilled haloumi for fresh feta.

Sticky Lamb Ribs

1oz/30g butter

2 cloves garlic, crushed

1 cup tomato sauce

¼ cup Worcestershire sauce

⅓ cup malt vinegar

⅓ cup brown sugar

1 teaspoon sweet chilli sauce (see page 82)

¼ teaspoon crushed black peppercorns

4lb/2kg lamb ribs, trimmed

1 Light the barbecue. Melt the butter in a frying pan over gentle heat, add the garlic and cook for 1 minute. Stir in the tomato sauce, Worcestershire sauce, vinegar, sugar, chilli sauce and pepper. Mix well then simmer, uncovered, for 10 minutes.

2 Barbecue the ribs over moderately hot coals until tender, brushing liberally at frequent intervals with the tomato sauce mixture. Serve with classic summer pasta salad (see page 69).

>
VARIATIONS
- This sticky sauce also goes well with chicken wings cooked in the same way.

Moroccan Lamb Skewers

3lb/1½ kg boneless lamb leg, cut into
    1in/2½cm cubes

2 onions, quartered

2 green peppers, cut into squares

GINGER AND CUMIN MARINADE

    ⅓ cup lemon juice

    2 tablespoons olive oil

    1 small onion, grated

    1 teaspoon salt

    1 teaspoon ground cumin

    ½in/1cm piece fresh ginger, grated

    freshly ground black pepper

1 To make the marinade, place the lemon juice, oil, onion, salt, cumin, ginger and black pepper in a ceramic or glass bowl and mix to combine. Add the lamb to marinade, stir to coat well and refrigerate for at least 2 hours.

2 Separate the onion quarters into petals. Thread the meat onto skewers alternately with pepper squares and onion pieces, not too closely together.

3 Cook the kebabs over hot coals, turning frequently, for 8–10 minutes or until lamb is crispy brown on the outside but still pink in the centre.

While waiting for this dish to cook, serve your guests some smoky eggplant dip (see page 82).

VARIATIONS

- This marinade also works well with beef.

- Other vegetables, such as red pepper, button mushrooms or zucchini slices, can be added to the skewers for extra colour and flavour.

Greek Barbecued Lamb Chops

½ cup olive oil

2 tablespoons lemon juice

1 onion, roughly chopped

2 teaspoons fresh oregano

2 bay leaves

6 lamb loin chops

¼ cup mixed fresh herbs

1. Combine the oil and lemon juice. Process the onion with oregano in a food processor, then stir into the oil mixture and add bay leaves. Arrange the chops in a single layer in a dish, pour over the marinade, cover and refrigerate for 30 minutes.

2. Light the barbecue to get to a medium heat. Remove the bay leaves from marinade, then barbecue chops until tender, basting frequently with the marinade. Garnish with fresh herbs and serve with grilled eggplant (see page 76).

> VARIATIONS

- Substitute the lamb with pork loin chops and serve with grilled green apple rings.

- Try this recipe with 6 boneless chicken thighs and cook some red pepper with the eggplant.

Lamb Fillet with Mango and Mint Chutney

¼ cup mint sauce

2 tablespoons olive oil

2 cloves garlic, crushed

2 tablespoons honey

1½lb/750g lamb fillets, trimmed

handful of watercress

MINT CHUTNEY

¾ cup chicken stock

¼ cup mango chutney

2 tablespoons mint jelly

1 tablespoon cider vinegar

2 teaspoons cornflour, dissolved in 1 tablespoon cold water

1 To make the mint chutney, combine the chicken stock, mango chutney, mint jelly, vinegar and cornflour mixture in a small saucepan over low heat. Bring to the boil, stirring constantly. Lower the heat and simmer until slightly thickened, then keep hot.

2 Light the barbecue. Combine the mint sauce, oil, garlic and honey in a small bowl and mix well. Cook the lamb fillets over moderately hot coals until tender, turning regularly and basting with the mint sauce mixture.

3 When cooked to your liking, transfer the lamb to a board, cut into slices and serve with watercress, mint chutney and barbecue corn cobs (see page 77).

VARIATIONS

• This dish is also lovely made with chicken fillets instead of lamb and sweet chilli sauce (see page 82) instead of both the mint sauce and mint jelly.

• Try this marinade and sauce with pork chops.

Rosemary Lamb Skewers

4 lamb back straps, cut into 1in/2½cm cubes

2 large onions, cut into eighths

ROSEMARY MARINADE

½ cup olive oil

2 cloves garlic, finely chopped

¼ cup fresh rosemary, chopped

freshly ground black pepper

½ cup lemon juice

1 Whisk the marinade ingredients together. Place the lamb cubes in a single layer in a dish, add the onions and marinade and toss to coat. Cover and refrigerate for at least 8 hours, stirring occasionally.

2. Light the barbecue. Thread the lamb and onion onto oiled metal skewers. Cook over hot coals until browned and tender, basting frequently with marinade.

Serve some grilled garlic bread (see page 78) while you wait for the lamb skewers.

VARIATIONS

• This recipe works well with chicken instead of lamb. Diced vegetables, such as peppers and zucchini, can be added to the skewers for extra colour and flavour.

Mustard Pork Spare Ribs

2lb/1kg pork spare ribs
¼ cup fresh rosemary, chopped
4 cloves garlic, finely chopped
salt and freshly ground black pepper

MUSTARD GLAZE
⅓ cup soft dark brown sugar
½ cup wholegrain mustard
⅓ cup cider vinegar
1 tablespoon mustard powder

1 To make the mustard glaze, combine sugar, wholegrain mustard, vinegar and mustard powder in a saucepan. Bring to a simmer, stirring constantly, then cool, cover and refrigerate overnight.

2 Light the barbecue. Rub the spare ribs with rosemary, garlic, salt and pepper. Place on the barbecue, cover and cook for 1 hour, turning once. Allow to cool.

3 Spread the meaty side of ribs with glaze. Cook skin-side down over hot coals until skin is crisp, then turn. Cook, brushing with the remaining glaze, until the ribs are crisp and glazed all over. Serve with wholegrain mustard potatoes (see page 78).

VARIATIONS

• Substitute honey or maple syrup for the brown sugar to get a different flavour.

• This sticky mustard glaze also works well on grilled chicken wings.

serves 6

Pork Kebabs with Peppers and Onions

1½lb/750g pork fillet, trimmed and cut into
   1in/2½cm cubes

¼ cup olive oil

1 tablespoon red wine vinegar

¼ small bunch fresh chives, chopped

salt and freshly ground black pepper

2 red peppers, cut into 1in/2½cm squares

2 yellow peppers, cut into 1in/2½cm squares

2 onions, cut into eighths, layers separated

1 Spread out the pork cubes in a single layer in a shallow dish. Whisk the oil, vinegar and chives in a bowl, add salt and pepper to taste and pour over the meat. Mix well, cover and marinate for 1 hour.

2 Light the barbecue. Drain the meat, discarding the marinade. Thread the pork cubes, pepper and onion pieces alternately onto oiled metal skewers. Cook over hot coals until tender, turning once. Serve with warm bean salad (see page 72).

> **VARIATIONS**
> • This recipe also works well with lamb instead of pork. Other vegetables, such as button mushrooms and zucchini slices, can be added to the skewers for extra colour and flavour.

Spicy Pork Bites

1½ cups natural yoghurt

1 onion, finely chopped

2 cloves garlic, crushed

1 tablespoon sweet chilli sauce

1 tablespoon freshly squeezed lime juice

1 teaspoon ground cumin

¼ cup fresh coriander, chopped

1lb/500g pork fillet, trimmed and cut into
  1in/2½cm cubes

⅓ cup dried apricots

1 Combine the yoghurt, onion, garlic, sweet chilli sauce, lime juice, cumin and coriander in a bowl and mix well.

2 Arrange the pork cubes in a single layer in a large shallow dish. Add the apricots then the yoghurt mixture, mix well, cover and refrigerate for 6 hours or overnight.

3 Light the barbecue. Drain the pork and apricots, reserving the marinade. Thread the pork cubes and apricots alternately onto oiled metal or soaked wooden skewers. Cook the skewers, turning occasionally and basting with marinade, until pork is cooked and apricots are tender. Serve with roasted whole onion and potato salad (see page 71).

VARIATIONS

• Substitute dried apple pieces for the dried apricots. This recipe also works well with diced chicken fillets.

Zesty Marinated Pork Cutlets

3in/8cm piece fresh ginger, finely chopped

2 cloves garlic, crushed

⅓ cup brown sugar

3 tablespoons Dijon mustard

¼ cup cider vinegar

juice of 2 limes

⅓ cup olive oil

salt and freshly ground black pepper

8 pork cutlets

1. Whisk the ginger, garlic, sugar, mustard, vinegar, lime juice, oil, salt and pepper together. Arrange the cutlets in a single layer in a dish, pour over ginger mixture, cover and marinate overnight in the refrigerator.

2. Cook the pork over hot coals, basting frequently with the marinade, until tender. Serve with honey baked carrots (see page 80).

> VARIATIONS
> • Substitute the pork with chicken fillets and use honey instead of the brown sugar.

Chinese Barbecued Pork Spare Ribs

2lb/1kg pork spare ribs

CHINESE BARBECUE MARINADE

1 tablespoon salted black beans

2 tablespoons dry sherry

1 tablespoon oyster sauce

1 tablespoon light soy sauce

2 teaspoons Chinese five-spice powder

freshly ground black pepper

1 cup spicy dark plum dipping sauce (see page 83)

1   To make the marinade, place black beans in a bowl, cover with a little water and set aside to stand for 10 minutes. Drain the beans and return to the bowl, mash with a fork and stir in the sherry, oyster sauce, soy sauce, five-spice powder and black pepper. Trim the excess fat from ribs. Coat the ribs well with marinade and allow to stand for 10–15 minutes.

2   Light the barbecue. Drain the ribs and discard the marinade. Cook over moderately low coals for 5 minutes on each side.

3   Brush with a little of the plum sauce and cook 5–10 minutes longer, turning once, until ribs are tender and glazed. Cut the ribs into small sections and serve with remaining plum sauce.

> VARIATIONS
- This marinade also goes well on pork chops or chicken wings.

Pork Chops with Mango Salsa

4 pork loin chops
salt and freshly ground black pepper
1 tablespoon vegetable oil
2 cloves garlic, crushed
1 tablespoon Worcestershire sauce
½ teaspoon mustard powder
1oz/30g butter, melted

SALSA
1 mango, stoned, peeled and diced
1 small red onion, finely diced
¼ cup fresh coriander, chopped
2 tablespoons olive oil
1 tablespoon lemon or lime juice
salt and freshly ground black pepper

1 Use a sharp knife to cut through the fat around the chops at 1in/2½cm intervals. Season to taste with salt and black pepper. Place the oil, garlic, Worcestershire sauce and mustard in a screw-top jar and shake well to combine. Brush the oil mixture over chops on both sides.

2 Light the barbecue. Place the chops on the barbecue and cook, brushing with butter every 2 minutes, for 6 minutes or until cooked through and tender.

3 While the chops are cooking, prepare the salsa. Combine the mango, onion and coriander in a bowl with the oil, lemon or lime juice and salt and pepper. Serve the chops with a generous spoon of mango salsa and foil barbecue potatoes with herb butter (see page 77).

---- VARIATIONS ----
- Use lemon juice instead of the Worcestershire sauce and use this recipe for fish cutlets instead of pork.

- Replace the mango with two diced tomatoes and the coriander with fresh basil.

Bacon and Chorizo Sausage Kebabs

4 chorizo sausages

8 rindless streaky bacon rashers

1 red pepper, cut into eight 1in/2½cm squares

12 button mushrooms

8 cherry tomatoes

8 shallots, peeled

2oz/60g butter, softened

1 tablespoon Dijon mustard

1 teaspoon lemon juice

1 Cut each chorizo sausage into 4. Spear the end of a bacon rasher with a long, oiled skewer. Add a chorizo piece, weave the bacon around and pierce the bacon again. Add a red pepper square, a mushroom, a tomato, a shallot and another sausage in the same way, then introduce another bacon rasher and repeat the sequence, ending with an extra mushroom. Make three more kebabs in the same way.

2 Melt the butter, mustard and lemon juice in a small saucepan, stirring constantly, then brush the mixture over the kebabs. Cook over hot coals, turning occasionally, until the bacon is crisp and the sausages are cooked through. Serve at once with sweet-and-sour barbecue sauce (see page 84).

❯

VARIATIONS

- Substitute vegetarian sausages and cubes of firm tofu for the bacon and chorizo for a great vegetarian meal.

serves 4

Chicken Pesto Burger

½ bunch fresh basil leaves

2 tablespoons pine nuts

½oz/15g Parmesan cheese, grated

1 clove garlic, crushed

2 tablespoons olive oil

1lb/500g chicken mince

1 cup breadcrumbs

1 red pepper, roasted and diced

1 onion, diced

1 egg white

freshly ground black pepper

4 rolls, split and toasted

4oz/125g rocket or watercress

1 tomato, sliced

1   Light the barbecue. To make the patties, place the basil, pine nuts, Parmesan, garlic and oil in a food processor or blender and process until smooth. Transfer the mixture to a bowl, add chicken, breadcrumbs, red pepper, onion, egg white and black pepper and mix well to combine.

2   Shape the chicken mixture into four patties. Place on the barbecue and cook for 3 minutes each side or until cooked. To serve, top the bottom half of each roll with rocket or watercress, then with a patty, tomato slices and top half of roll. Serve immediately.

While you are waiting for this to cook, serve your guests spicy barbecue beer nuts (see page 81).

Notes: Peppers are easy to roast on the barbecue – remove seeds, cut into quarters and place skin-side down on a preheated hot barbecue. Cook until skins are charred and blistered, then place in a plastic food bag and set aside until cool enough to handle. Remove skin and use as desired.

VARIATIONS

• You could use pork mince instead of chicken mince.

• Substitute the chicken with white fish and place this in a food processor with ½ bunch coriander, 1 tablespoon freshly chopped ginger and 1 clove crushed garlic, then continue the recipe from step 2.

Yakitori Chicken Skewers

2lb/1kg boneless chicken, cut into 1in/2½cm cubes

1 bunch spring onions, cut into 2in/5cm lengths

2 green or red peppers, cut into 2in/5cm squares

SOY AND SAKE MARINADE

¾ cup soy sauce

¾ cup sake or mirin

¼ cup sugar

1 pinch powdered sansho or ground pepper

1   Thread the chicken, spring onions and green or red peppers alternately onto 8 skewers and arrange in a single layer in a shallow glass or ceramic dish. Place the soy sauce, sake or mirin and sugar in a bowl and mix well to dissolve sugar. Pour the mixture over the skewers, cover and set aside to marinate for 30 minutes, turning occasionally.

2   Light the barbecue. Drain the skewers, reserving the marinade. Cook on the barbecue for 3 minutes, dip skewers into the marinade, turn and cook for 2 minutes more or until tender and glazed. Serve hot with a pinch of sansho or pepper and bacon roasted potatoes (see page 80).

Note: Sansho is available in powdered form from Japanese or oriental food stores. It has a fragrant peppery taste.

> VARIATIONS

• You can replace the chicken with firm white fish or prawns, or both!

serves 4

Oriental Barbecued Chicken Wings

2lb/1kg chicken wings, wing tips removed

FIVE-SPICE MARINADE
- ½ small onion, finely chopped
- 1 clove garlic, crushed
- 2 tablespoons soy sauce
- 1 tablespoon honey
- 1 tablespoon tomato sauce
- 1 tablespoon vegetable oil
- 1 teaspoon Chinese five-spice powder

1 To make the marinade, place the onion, garlic, soy sauce, honey, tomato sauce, oil and five-spice powder in a large bowl and mix to combine. Add the wings, turning to coat, cover and marinate for several hours or overnight in the refrigerator.

2 Drain the wings and cook on the barbecue, turning and basting frequently with marinade, for 10–15 minutes or until brown and crisp. Heat the remaining marinade to serve as a dipping sauce with the wings. Serve with warm bean salad (see page 72).

❯

VARIATIONS
- This recipe also works well with pork chops instead of chicken wings.

Mediterranean Barbecued Chicken

4 tablespoons lemon juice
½ onion, finely chopped
2 tablespoons olive oil
2 cloves garlic, crushed
¼ cup fresh oregano
salt and freshly ground black pepper
2 small chickens, quartered

1 Combine the lemon juice, onion, oil, garlic, oregano, salt and black pepper in a large shallow glass dish. Add the chicken, turning to coat, and set aside to marinate for at least 1 hour.

2 Light the barbecue. Drain the chicken, reserving the marinade, then place skin-side down on the barbecue and cook for 5 minutes. Turn, baste with the marinade, and cook for 10 minutes more. Turn and cook for 5 minutes longer or until chicken is tender and juices run clear when pierced. Serve on a bed of mixed greens.

Serve some barbecued mushrooms with chilli butter (see page 79) while you wait for the chicken.

VARIATIONS

• Try this recipe with 4 small racks of lamb, each halved. Add olives and feta to the salad greens.

Barbecued Chicken Burger with Aïoli (Garlic Mayonnaise)

4 chicken fillets

½ cup olive oil

¼ cup lemon juice

4 burger buns, split

2 tomatoes, sliced

large handful of fresh lettuce

1 lemon, cut into wedges

¼ cup fresh parsley, chopped

AÏOLI

2 egg yolks

¼ cup fresh parsley, chopped

¼ small bunch fresh chives, chopped

2 tablespoons lemon juice

4 cloves garlic, crushed

1¼ cups olive oil

salt and freshly ground black pepper

1 Arrange the chicken fillets in a single layer in a shallow bowl. Mix the oil and lemon juice together, pour the mixture over the chicken, cover and marinate for 1 hour.

2 To make the aïoli, combine the egg yolks, fresh herbs, lemon juice and crushed garlic in a blender or food processor. Process briefly to blend. With the motor running, gradually add the oil, drop by drop, then in a steady stream, until the mixture thickens to the consistency of mayonnaise. Transfer to a bowl and add salt and pepper to taste.

3 Barbecue the chicken over hot coals until tender, basting frequently with the oil and lemon juice mixture. On the bottom of each burger bun place tomato slices and fresh lettuce, top with chicken and bun lid. Garnish with lemon wedges and chopped parsley and serve with the aïoli.

Serve some warm marinated olives (see page 81) while you wait for these burgers.

>

VARIATIONS

• Substitute firm white fish fillets for the chicken. To make tartare sauce, omit the garlic from the aïoli, add 1 teaspoon of chopped capers and 1 chopped gherkin with the salt and pepper, and serve with the fish burgers.

Honey and Ginger Drumsticks

¼ cup honey
2 teaspoons ground ginger
¼ cup Worcestershire sauce
2 tablespoons soy sauce
2 cloves garlic, crushed
3lb/1½kg chicken drumsticks

1 Heat the honey, ginger, Worcestershire sauce, soy sauce and garlic together in a small saucepan. When the mixture boils, remove from the heat.

2 Light the barbecue and brush the chicken drumsticks generously with the honey ginger mixture. Barbecue the drumsticks, basting frequently with the honey ginger mixture, until tender and cooked through. Serve with classic summer pasta salad (see page 69).

›

VARIATIONS

• You can use this sauce to baste fish cutlets by substituting fresh ginger for the ground ginger and lime juice for the Worcestershire sauce.

seafood

Catch of the Day

serves 4

Ginger and Soy Prawn Skewers

2lb/1kg peeled raw prawns

SOY GINGER MARINADE

¼ cup dry vermouth

¼ cup soy sauce

1 tablespoon soft brown sugar

3in/8cm piece fresh ginger, grated

¼ teaspoon freshly ground black pepper

1 To make the marinade, place the vermouth, soy sauce, sugar, ginger and pepper in a deep bowl and mix to combine. Place the prawns in the marinade, turn to coat well and set aside to marinate, turning once or twice, for 30 minutes.

2 Light the barbecue. Drain the prawns well, reserving marinade, and thread onto skewers. Cook over hot coals, turning and basting with marinade, for 2 minutes each side.

❯

VARIATIONS

- This marinade also works well with diced chicken or pork.
- Substitute half the prawns for other seafood and skewer alternately with the prawns.

Barbecued Calamari Strips

1lb/500g small calamari, prepared and ready
 to cook

½ cup olive oil

½ teaspoon ground paprika

few drops of Tabasco

salt and freshly ground black pepper

½ cup fresh parsley, chopped

2 lemons, quartered

1 Cut the calamari lengthwise into 2 or 4 pieces,
 or into fine strips or rings, and place in a bowl
 – leave whole if very small. Add the oil, paprika
 and Tabasco and mix well. Season to taste with
 salt and black pepper and set aside to marinate,
 stirring occasionally, for 2 hours.

2 Cook the calamari with the marinade on the
 barbecue over hot coals, turning often, for
 3–4 minutes or until opaque. Take care not to
 overcook. Sprinkle with parsley, garnish with
 lemon quarters and serve immediately with sweet
 potato salad with pine nuts (see page 68).

*Note: Choose small calamari for this quick cooking
method and serve as soon as they turn opaque,
as the flesh toughens on standing.*

〉

VARIATIONS

- This recipe works really well if you use fresh
 prawns instead of calamari and substitute a small,
 chopped red chilli for the Tabasco and coriander
 for the parsley.

- You can also try this recipe with scallops instead
 of calamari.

Sesame Prawn Cakes

10½oz/300g peeled raw prawns

9oz/250g fresh crab meat

3 spring onions, chopped

¼ cup fresh basil, finely chopped

1 fresh red chilli, finely chopped

1 teaspoon ground cumin

1 teaspoon ground paprika

1 egg white

5½oz/150g sesame seeds

1 tablespoon vegetable oil

1 Light the barbecue. Place the prawns, crab meat, spring onions, basil, chilli, cumin, paprika and egg white in a food processor and process until well combined. Take 4 tablespoons of the mixture, shape into a patty and roll in sesame seeds to coat. Repeat with the remaining mixture to make six patties.

2 Cook the patties on the barbecue for 10 minutes each side or until golden and cooked. Serve with sweet chilli sauce (see page 82).

> **VARIATIONS**
> - You could use 19½oz/550g of chicken mince instead of the prawns and crab meat.
> - To serve as an appetiser, roll heaped teaspoonfuls of the mixture in sesame seeds and cook for 2–3 minutes each side, then serve with sweet chilli sauce.

Scallops with Plum Glaze

24oz/680g scallops

¼ cup chilli plum marinade (see page 84)

1 Wash and clean the scallops, then thread evenly onto 8 skewers. Place the scallops on the barbecue and baste with plum marinade.

2 Cook for a minute each side, basting with the marinade when you turn them. Serve with extra, warmed chilli plum marinade.

>

---- VARIATIONS ----
- You could use this recipe with diced chicken or pork.

serves 4–6

Marinated Swordfish Steaks

2 cloves garlic, finely chopped

½ cup lemon juice

2 fresh red chillies, finely chopped

2 teaspoons honey

¾ cup fresh coriander, chopped

2lb/1kg swordfish steaks

1 Mix the garlic, lemon juice, chillies, honey and ½ cup coriander in a bowl and combine well. Add the swordfish steaks and spoon over marinade. Allow to marinate for 2 hours.

2 Cook the steaks on the barbecue, turning occasionally and basting with the marinade, until cooked. Sprinkle with remaining coriander. Serve with lemon wedges and avocado salsa (see page 82) on the side.

Note: Although swordfish is used in this recipe, you can easily replace it with other firm-textured fish, for example, tuna.

> VARIATIONS

- This marinade also works well with chicken fillets.
- For a milder marinade, leave out the chilli and add some other fresh herbs or some finely grated fresh ginger.

Charcoal-Grilled Prawns

2lb/1kg raw medium prawns
1½in/4cm piece fresh ginger, finely chopped
¼ cup fresh parsley, finely chopped
1 bay leaf
1 sprig fresh thyme, chopped
¼ teaspoon dried, crushed red chillies
salt and freshly ground black pepper
2 tablespoons olive oil
2 tablespoons fresh lemon juice
3oz/85g butter
1 clove garlic, crushed

1 Using kitchen shears, cut along the back of each prawn, rub gently under cold running water to remove black vein, then pat dry on absorbent paper. It's best not to peel the prawns, but if you do peel them, leave tail segments intact.

2 Place the prawns in a large bowl, sprinkle with ginger, parsley, bay leaf, thyme, dried chillies, salt and black pepper. Add the oil and lemon juice, mix well and set aside to marinate for 30 minutes.

3 Light the barbecue. Drain the prawns and place over moderately hot coals and cook for 2 minutes. Turn and cook 2–3 minutes longer or until prawns curl and turn pink. Melt the butter with garlic in a small saucepan. When bubbling, discard the garlic, pour over prawns and serve immediately.

Serve your guests some barbecued mushrooms with chilli butter (see page 79) while you wait for this dish.

>

---- VARIATIONS ----

• Try this recipe with lobster for a special occasion. Boil 3 lobsters for 5 minutes, cut them in half, mix through the marinade and grill until cooked. Serve with the butter.

serves 4

Barbecued Sardines

24 fresh sardines, cleaned

salt and freshly ground black pepper

3 tablespoons lemon juice

¼ cup olive oil

1½ cups breadcrumbs

¼ cup fresh parsley, chopped

3 lemons, quartered

1   Place the sardines in a bowl with salt and black pepper to taste. Add lemon juice and oil and lightly mix to coat. Set aside to marinate for 30 minutes.

2   Drain and roll the sardines in breadcrumbs, pressing firmly to coat. Place over hot coals and cook for 2–3 minutes on each side, or until cooked through and golden. Sprinkle with parsley and serve immediately with lemon wedges and tabbouleh salad (see page 74).

Note: Look for small sardines about 4in/10cm long and cook them whole. If using larger fish, remove the heads then slit the stomach and remove entrails before cooking, or buy the fish prepared from a fishmonger.

> VARIATIONS
> - Instead of sardines, you can use scallops or a mixture of seafood, including peeled prawns, scallops and small pieces of fish.

serves 4

Seafood Kebabs

12 scallops, rinsed

12 raw king prawns, peeled, tails intact

2 firm fish fillets, cut into 1in/2½ cm cubes

2oz/60g butter

¼ cup lemon juice

1 clove garlic, crushed

¼ teaspoon freshly ground black pepper

¼ cup each fresh parsley, chives and thyme, chopped

1 Thread the scallops onto 4 skewers, the prawns onto 4 skewers, and the fish cubes onto 4 skewers.

2 Melt the butter in a small saucepan. Stir in the lemon juice, garlic and pepper, then brush each kebab generously with the mixture. Sprinkle parsley over the scallops, chives over the prawns and thyme over the fish cubes.

3 Grill the kebabs over moderately hot coals for about 2 minutes each side or until tender. Serve with Caesar salad (see page 70).

> VARIATIONS

• Vary the fish and seafood in this recipe according to what's in season and your own preferences.

• A finely sliced red chilli added to the melted butter will give this dish an extra kick.

serves 4

Barbecued Tuna Steaks

1½lb/750g fresh tuna
¼ cup vegetable oil
2 tablespoons white vinegar
salt
4 sprigs fresh thyme
¼ cup fresh parsley, chopped

1   Trim any dark flesh from the tuna and cut into 4 steaks. Place the oil, vinegar and salt in a shallow glass dish and mix to combine. Add the tuna steaks, turning to coat, and set aside to marinate for 1 hour.

2   Drain the tuna, reserving the marinade. With the thyme sprigs, place steaks in a fish grill on the barbecue over moderately hot coals. Cook, basting with the marinade, for 3–5 minutes each side or until golden and flesh flakes easily. Sprinkle with parsley and serve with classic potato and egg salad (see page 73).

VARIATIONS

• Peel, deseed and dice 1lb/500g tomatoes, mix these with some salt and pepper, 2 tablespoons lemon juice and 3 tablespoons olive oil. Cook the tuna steaks as above, then slice, arrange on a serving plate and spoon over tomato mixture. Garnish with fresh, chopped herbs.

Barbecued Spiced Fish Fillets

4 firm white fish fillets

2 tablespoons Worcestershire sauce

2 tablespoons olive oil

2 teaspoons soy sauce

½ teaspoon chilli powder

2 cloves garlic, crushed

dash of Tabasco

1 Arrange the fish fillets in a dish large enough to hold them in a single layer. Mix the remaining ingredients in a small bowl, pour over the fish, cover and marinate for 1 hour.

2 Cook the fish over moderately hot coals, basting frequently with marinade, until tender. Serve with classic summer pasta salad (see page 69).

VARIATIONS

- Fresh chopped herbs and a good squeeze of lemon juice can be added just as the fish finishes cooking for an extra zing.

serves 4

Golden Grilled Sea Bass

4 sea bass fillets, about 5½ oz/150g each

½oz/15g butter, melted

2 tomatoes, peeled, deseeded and diced

4 tablespoons mayonnaise

salt and freshly ground black pepper

1 Brush the fish with melted butter. Place on the barbecue over hot coals, skin-side down, and cook for 3–4 minutes.

2 Turn the fish over, top with tomatoes and mayonnaise and cook for 3–4 minutes longer, or until golden brown and flesh flakes easily. Season to taste with salt and black pepper and serve with sweet potato salad with pine nuts (see page 68).

Note: To peel and deseed a tomato, cut the core out of the top of the tomato with a small knife, then lightly cut a cross through the skin on the bottom of the tomato. Place into a deep bowl or jug and pour boiling water over until tomatoes are covered. Leave for 60 seconds, then drain, rinse under cold water and peel away the skin. Next, cut the tomato in half horizontally and use your fingers to scoop out the seeds. Dice flesh and use as required.

>

VARIATIONS

- Mix the diced tomato with some finely diced red onion and chopped fresh basil for extra flavour.
- You could use chicken fillets instead of sea bass.

serves 4

Salmon Steaks with Lime Butter

3oz/85g butter

1 clove garlic, crushed

¼ cup freshly squeezed lime juice

grated zest of 2 limes

grated zest of 1 lemon

1 tablespoon dry white wine

2 teaspoons honey

¼ cup fresh parsley, chopped

4 salmon or other firm fish fillets, about 7oz/200g each

1   Melt the butter in a small saucepan over moderate heat. Stir in the garlic and cook for 1 minute. Add the lime juice, lime zest, lemon zest, wine and honey and mix well. Stir in the parsley.

2   Cook the fish over moderately hot coals, brushing frequently with the lime butter baste, for about 3 minutes on each side or until cooked through. Serve with classic potato and egg salad (see page 73).

VARIATIONS

• This butter also works very well with chicken. Use lemon juice if you can't find fresh limes. The addition of some finely sliced fresh chilli will give the dish an extra kick.

serves 4

Barbecued Mustard-Marinated Fish Cutlets

2 tablespoons wholegrain mustard
1 tablespoon honey
¼ cup dry white wine
1 clove garlic, crushed
4 fish cutlets, about 6½oz/185g each

1   Combine the mustard, honey, wine and garlic in a shallow bowl and mix well. Turn the cutlets in the mixture until coated on both sides. Set aside for 30 minutes to marinate.

2   Cook the fish over moderately hot coals until tender. Serve with wholegrain mustard potatoes (see page 78).

> VARIATIONS

- Varying the type of mustard in this marinade will give you different flavours.
- This marinade also works well with pork cutlets.

Tuna with Wasabi and Sweet Soy

2 tuna steaks, about 1in/2½cm thick and 1lb/500g each

GRILLING SAUCE
- ½ cup soy sauce
- ½ cup mirin or sake
- 2 tablespoons sugar
- ½ teaspoon wasabi paste or powder

1 To make the sauce, combine the soy sauce, mirin or sake, sugar and wasabi in a saucepan and stir over low heat until sugar dissolves and the mixture comes to the boil.

2 Light the barbecue. Coat the tuna steaks with the grilling sauce and cook, turning and basting occasionally, until steaks are done to your liking.

3 Slice the steaks into thick slices, place on top of salad greens and garnish with sliced spring onions. Serve remaining sauce on the side.

Note: Serve your guests some barbecue potato skins (see page 79) and smoky eggplant dip (see page 82) while you prepare this dish.

VARIATIONS

- This recipe also works well with thick steaks of good-quality beef. Shave some cucumber and carrot with a vegetable peeler and add it to the salad.

Straight from the Garden

Vege Burgers with Sweet Chilli Sauce

1lb/500g broccoli, chopped

1lb/500g zucchini, chopped

½lb/250g carrots, chopped

2 onions, finely chopped

2 cloves garlic, crushed

½ cup fresh parsley, chopped

3 cups dried breadcrumbs

½ cup plain flour, sifted

freshly ground black pepper

10 wholemeal rolls, split

10 lettuce leaves

1 cucumber, shaved into ribbons with a
    vegetable peeler

1 cup sweet chilli sauce (see page 82)

1   Boil or steam the broccoli, zucchini and carrots until tender. Drain, rinse under cold running water and pat dry.

2   Place the broccoli, zucchini, carrots, onions, garlic and parsley in a food processor and process until puréed. Transfer the vegetable mixture to a mixing bowl, add breadcrumbs and flour, season with black pepper and mix to combine. Cover and refrigerate for 30 minutes.

3   Shape the mixture into ten patties. Place on a non-stick baking tray, cover and refrigerate until required.

4   Light the barbecue. Cook the patties on the barbecue for 3–4 minutes each side. Toast the rolls on the barbecue. Place a lettuce leaf, a patty, some cucumber and a spoonful of chilli sauce on the bottom half of each roll, top with remaining roll half and serve immediately with extra chilli sauce.

>

VARIATIONS

- Replace the broccoli with 500g canned, drained, mixed beans.

- If your guests are not vegan, cheese makes a lovely addition. Place a slice of tasty cheese on each patty near the end of cooking and allow it to melt before serving.

Vegetarian Sausages

2 cups cooked cannellini beans

½ cup wholemeal breadcrumbs

1 small onion, minced

1 clove garlic, minced

¼ cup tomato sauce

1 egg or equivalent in egg-replacer

¼ cup fresh basil, chopped

¼ cup fresh parsley, chopped

⅛ teaspoon ground cumin

⅛ teaspoon dried chilli

salt

1 Combine the beans, breadcrumbs, onion, garlic, tomato sauce, egg, herbs and spices and mix until well combined.

2 Light the barbecue. Shape small handfuls of the mixture into sausages and place gently on the barbecue. Cook, turning carefully, until golden. Serve in hot dog rolls with home-made tomato sauce (see page 83).

> **VARIATIONS**
>
> • If you wish, this mixture can be made into patties and used for vegetarian burgers instead.
>
> • Add extra flavour to this mixture with ¼ cup minced olives or sun-dried tomatoes.

Barbecued Noodles

1lb/500g egg noodles

¼ cup fresh coriander, chopped

½in/1cm piece fresh ginger, chopped

1 clove garlic, crushed

1 small fresh chilli, deseeded and chopped

1 medium onion, sliced

1 cup broccoli florets

1 medium red pepper, cut into strips

1 cup baby spinach

1 bunch asparagus, sliced

2 tablespoons vegetarian oyster sauce

2 tablespoons sweet chilli sauce (see page 82)

1 Rinse noodles in hot water, separate and drain very well. Mix coriander, ginger, garlic, chilli and onion.

2. Heat the barbecue hotplate or use a tin baking dish on grill plate. Oil hotplate or dish, add the onion mixture and cook until they begin to soften.

3 Add the vegetables and noodles, toss around to mix well and heat through. At the last minute, add the oyster and sweet chilli sauces, toss quickly to combine and serve immediately.

While you prepare this dish, serve your guests some smoky eggplant dip (see page 82) and warm marinated olives (see page 81).

Note: If you do not have a hotplate, cook these inside with a frying pan and bring them out to the barbecue.

> VARIATIONS

- This dish can be varied easily by adding different vegetables, for example, carrots, zucchini, cauliflower or mushrooms.
- Firm, diced tofu also goes well in this dish. Fry the tofu on the grill with the onion mixture and continue the recipe as above.

Barbecued Summer Vegetables

1 eggplant, thickly sliced lengthwise

2 onions, thickly sliced

2 large tomatoes, halved

3–4 zucchini, sliced lengthwise

6½ oz/185g flat mushrooms

SEASONED OIL

¼ cup olive oil

2 cloves garlic, crushed

¼ small onion, finely chopped

½ teaspoon salt

1 fresh red chilli, chopped (optional)

1   To make the oil, place the, garlic, onion, salt, oil and chilli (if using) in a screw-top jar and shake well to combine. Set aside to stand for several hours to allow flavours to develop.

2   Place the vegetables and mushrooms on the barbecue over moderately hot coals, brush well with oil mixture and cook for 5 minutes. Turn, baste again and cook 2–3 minutes longer or until tender. Serve immediately with some bread and sweet potato salad with pine nuts (see page 68).

›

VARIATIONS

• Red, yellow or green pepper will add colour to this dish – simply cut the ends off the peppers, remove the seeds and membranes and cut the flesh into wide strips. Halved yellow baby squash also work well.

• These vegetables make a great accompaniment to barbecued tofu or vegetarian sausages.

Vegetable Kebabs with Home-Made Tomato Sauce

12 baby squash or 3 zucchini, cut into chunks

6 baby eggplant, cut into chunks

12 small onions, peeled

12 firm cherry tomatoes

12 button mushrooms

1 cup home-made tomato sauce (see page 83)

1 Preheat the barbecue. Thread the squash or zucchini, eggplant, onions, tomatoes and mushrooms onto lightly oiled skewers. Cook on the barbecue, turning frequently, for 5 minutes or until vegetables are golden and tender.

2 Warm tomato sauce and spoon over kebabs to serve.

❯

---- VARIATIONS ----

• The vegetables used in this recipe can be exchanged for others if you prefer – try cooked baby potatoes or baby beetroot, large diced pepper or canned artichoke hearts.

• For extra flavour, make a rosemary and garlic oil by adding 2 cloves of crushed garlic and a couple of stems of rosemary, gently bruised with the back of a knife, to ½ cup of olive oil. Allow to infuse for a few hours, then use to baste the skewers during cooking.

serves 4

Spring Vegetable Fritters

1 large carrot, grated

2 potatoes, grated and squeezed well to remove excess water

1 zucchini, grated

½ cup corn kernels

½ cup peas

1 egg, lightly beaten

1 tablespoon self-raising flour

¼ cup fresh parsley, finely chopped

¼ small bunch fresh chives, finely chopped

¼ teaspoon ground nutmeg

freshly ground black pepper

1 Mix all ingredients in a bowl.

2 Preheat the barbecue. Make heaped tablespoonfuls of mixture, flatten them slightly and cook on the barbecue 4–5 minutes each side or until golden brown.

3 Serve hot with salad and avocado salsa (see page 82).

VARIATIONS

• These fritters can be used as vegetarian burger patties. Serve in rolls with fresh salad and condiments.

• Exchange half the potato for sweet potato, cook heaped teaspoonfuls of the mixture and serve with mayonnaise as an appetiser.

serves 4

Stuffed Mediterranean Mushrooms

⅔ cup couscous

½ oz/15g butter

2 teaspoons olive oil

1 onion, chopped

2 cloves garlic, crushed

1 teaspoon garam masala

pinch of cayenne pepper

12 large mushrooms, stalks removed

7oz/200g feta cheese, crumbled

1 Light the barbecue to a high heat. Place the couscous in a bowl, pour over ⅔ cup boiling water, cover and set aside to stand for 5 minutes or until water is absorbed. Add the butter and toss gently with a fork.

2 Heat some oil in a frying pan over a medium heat, add onion and garlic and cook, stirring, for 3 minutes or until onion is soft. Add the garam masala and cayenne and cook for 1 minute longer. Add the onion mixture to couscous and toss to combine.

3 Fill the mushrooms with the couscous mixture, top with feta cheese and cook on barbecue for 5 minutes or until mushrooms are tender and cheese melts. Serve immediately with classic potato and egg salad (see page 73).

>

---- VARIATIONS ------------------------------

- Vary the flavour of the stuffing by adding fresh, chopped herbs, some chopped olives, sun-dried tomatoes or roasted pepper.

- Use 1½ cups cooked short-grain rice instead of the couscous to make this dish suitable for people with wheat allergies.

serves 4

Sweet Potato Salad with Pine Nuts

This recipe accompanies: Tandori beef ribs (See page 14); Barbecued calamari strips (See page 46); Golden grilled sea bass (See page 56); Barbecued summer vegetables (See page 64)

11oz/315g orange sweet potato, peeled and cut into 1in/2½cm-thick slices

6½ oz/185g white sweet potato, peeled and cut into 1in/2½cm-thick slices

2oz/60g butter

2 red onions, finely sliced

1½in/4cm piece fresh ginger, finely grated

1 tablespoon brown sugar

1 tablespoon red wine vinegar

¼ cup pine nuts, toasted

1 cup natural yoghurt

½ cup fresh parsley, chopped

1 Boil or steam the orange and white sweet potatoes until tender. Drain and set aside to cool.

2 Melt the butter in a frying pan, add onions, ginger, sugar and vinegar and cook, stirring, for 15 minutes or until onions start to caramelize. Remove pan from heat and set aside to cool.

3 Place sweet potatoes, onion mixture, pine nuts, yoghurt and parsley in a bowl and toss to combine.

❯

VARIATIONS

- Use regular potatoes instead of the sweet potatoes and add 2 tablespoons of chopped sun-dried tomatoes to the salad.

- Add a teaspoon of wholegrain mustard and a handful of chopped fresh basil to the dressing for a different flavour.

Classic Summer Pasta Salad

This recipe accompanies: Sticky lamb ribs (See page 25);
Honey and ginger drumsticks (See page 42); Barbecued spiced fish fillets
(See page 54)

13oz/375g pasta shapes

9oz/250g cherry tomatoes

4½oz/125g watercress

1 green pepper, chopped

2 tablespoons pine nuts

PESTO DRESSING

1 bunch fresh basil leaves

3 tablespoons pine nuts

¾ oz/20g Parmesan cheese, grated

1 clove garlic, crushed

½ cup mayonnaise

1 Bring a large saucepan of salted water to the boil, add the pasta and cook for 8 minutes or until just firm in the centre (al dente). Drain, rinse under cold running water and set aside to cool completely.

2 Place the pasta, tomatoes, watercress and green pepper in a salad bowl and toss to combine.

3 To make the dressing, place the basil, pine nuts, Parmesan, garlic, mayonnaise and 2 tablespoons water in a food processor or blender and process until smooth. Spoon the dressing over salad and sprinkle with remaining pine nuts.

Note: This salad looks pretty when made with bows, spirals or shells. Choose the pasta to suit the other dishes you are serving.

> **VARIATIONS**

- To add more colour to this dish, use a roasted, peeled and sliced red pepper instead of the green pepper.

- This salad is also lovely with 1lb/500g canned, drained, mixed beans in place of the pasta. This would also make it suitable for people with wheat allergies.

serves 10

Vegetarian Caesar Salad

This recipe goes well with Seafood kebabs (See page 52)

⅓ cup olive oil

2 slices bread, crusts removed and cut into ½in/1cm cubes

1 cos lettuce, washed, leaves separated and torn into large pieces

2oz/60g pine nuts, toasted

3 hard-boiled eggs, quartered

4½oz/125g Parmesan cheese, grated

DRESSING

1 egg yolk

¼ cup fresh parsley, chopped

¼ small bunch fresh chives, snipped

2 tablespoons lemon juice

⅔ cup olive oil

salt and freshly ground black pepper

1 To make the croutons, heat the oil in a frying pan and cook bread, tossing frequently, over a medium high heat for 1–2 minutes or until golden on all sides. Remove from pan and drain on absorbent paper.

2 To make the dressing, combine the egg yolk, fresh herbs and lemon juice in a blender or food processor. Process briefly to blend. With the motor running, gradually add the oil, drop by drop, then in a steady stream, until the mixture thickens to the consistency of mayonnaise. Transfer the dressing to a bowl and add salt and pepper to taste.

3 Place the lettuce, croutons and pine nuts in a serving bowl, pour dressing over and toss. Arrange egg quarters over salad, sprinkle with Parmesan and serve immediately.

VARIATIONS

• Add some grilled, sliced tofu to the salad when dressing.

Note: You can use iceberg lettuce in this recipe if cos lettuce is unavailable.

serves 6

Roasted Whole Onion and Potato Salad

This recipe goes well with spicy pork bites (See page 32)

2lb/1kg baby potatoes

12 baby onions, halved

¼cup olive oil

8 sprigs fresh rosemary

1 teaspoon sea salt

4 spring onions, chopped

MINT DRESSING

1 cup natural yoghurt

¼ cup mayonnaise

2 tablespoons wholegrain mustard

¼ cup fresh mint, chopped

1   Pre heat oven to 180°C. Bring a saucepan of water to the boil, add potatoes and onions, cook for 5 minutes, then drain well.

2   Place potatoes and onions in a lightly oiled roasting tin, brush with oil, scatter with rosemary and sprinkle with salt. Place the roasting tin in oven and cook, turning occasionally, for 20 minutes or until potatoes are tender.

3   To make dressing, place yoghurt, mayonnaise, mustard and mint in a bowl and mix to combine.

4   Drain oil from potato mixture and place potatoes and onions in a large salad bowl, then add spring onions. Spoon over dressing, toss to combine and serve immediately.

VARIATIONS

• Replace some of the potatoes in this recipe with baby carrots and baby beetroot for extra colour and variety.

• Use fresh basil instead of mint in the dressing, and add 2 tomatoes cut into wedges and a handful of olives to the salad when dressing.

serves 4

Warm Bean Salad

This recipe accompanies: Beef kebabs (See page 18); Pork kebabs with peppers and onions (See page 31); Oriental barbecued chicken wings (See page 39)

½lb/250g green beans, trimmed and cut into
    1in/2½cm lengths

½lb/250g canned kidney beans, drained and rinsed

½ red pepper, cut into very thin strips

zest and juice of 1 orange

2 tablespoons red wine vinegar

3 tablespoons olive oil

¼ teaspoon black peppercorns, crushed

4 sprigs fresh tarragon, finely chopped

1   Cook the green beans in a large saucepan of boiling water for about 3 minutes or until crisp-tender. Drain, refresh under cold running water, then drain again.

2   Tip the green beans into a salad bowl. Add the kidney beans, red pepper and orange zest.

3   Whisk the orange juice, vinegar, oil, crushed peppercorns and tarragon in a small bowl, pour over the salad and toss well.

VARIATIONS

• Add a handful of sun-dried tomatoes and 7oz/200g firm, diced tofu to this salad when assembling.

• Add a handful of black olives, 2 tomatoes cut into wedges and 2 hard-boiled eggs cut into quarters to the salad before dressing.

serves 6

Classic Potato and Egg Salad

This recipe accompanies: Charred t-bone steak with chilli herb butter (See page 12); Barbecued tuna steaks (See page 53); Salmon steaks with lime butter (See page 56); Stuffed Mediterranean mushrooms (See page 67)

10–12 small new potatoes

3 hard-boiled eggs, sliced

2 stalks celery, sliced

2 dill pickles, sliced

1 tablespoon capers

2 teaspoons horseradish cream

½ cup mayonnaise or sour cream

¼ bunch fresh chives, chopped

PARSLEY DRESSING

⅓ cup olive oil

2 tablespoons vinegar

¼ small onion, finely chopped

¼ cup fresh parsley, chopped

salt and freshly ground black pepper

1   Cook the potatoes in boiling salted water for 8–10 minutes or until just tender. Cut into thick slices or quarters while still warm.

2   To make the dressing, combine the oil, vinegar, onion and parsley in a large mixing bowl and whisk until thickened. Season to taste with salt and black pepper, then add warm potatoes and toss lightly to coat. Set aside to stand until cool.

3   Add the eggs, celery, pickles and capers to potatoes. Place horseradish cream and mayonnaise or sour cream in a small bowl, mix to combine and lightly fold through salad. Transfer to a serving bowl and sprinkle with chives.

VARIATIONS

• Replace the horseradish cream with wholegrain mustard and add a handful of olives and 2 tablespoons chopped sun-dried tomatoes to the salad when dressing.

Tabbouleh Salad

This recipe accompanies: Lamb souvlaki (See page 23);
Barbecued sardines (See page 51)

125g bulgar wheat
10 spring onions, finely chopped
1 bunch fresh flat-leaf parsley, chopped
¾ cup fresh mint, chopped
2 ripe tomatoes, chopped
¼ cup vegetable oil
¼ cup lemon juice
salt and freshly ground black pepper
lettuce leaves (optional)

1   Soak the wheat in cold water for 1 hour. Drain well
    and squeeze out excess liquid. Place wheat in a
    bowl, cover and refrigerate for 1 hour.

2   Add the spring onions to wheat and mix well,
    crushing with the back of a spoon to slightly bruise
    the onions. Add the parsley, mint, tomatoes, oil and
    lemon juice and mix thoroughly. Season to taste
    with salt and black pepper.

3   Line a salad bowl with lettuce leaves (if using) and
    spoon in the tabbouleh.

VARIATIONS

• Exchange the bulgar wheat for 1½ cups of
  cooked, long-grain rice and add ¼ cup of peas
  and ¼ cup corn kernels to the salad – this makes
  the salad suitable for people with wheat allergies.

All the Extras

Grilled Eggplant with Fresh Herbs

This recipe accompanies: Greek barbecued lamb chops (See page 27)

5 tablespoons olive oil

1 clove garlic, crushed

¼ teaspoon freshly ground black pepper

1 medium eggplant, cut into ½in/1cm slices

¼ cup fresh parsley, chopped

¼ cup fresh thyme, chopped

⅓ cup balsamic vinegar

1 Light the barbecue. Combine 3 tablespoons of the olive oil with the garlic and pepper. Brush the mixture over eggplant slices. Cook for 3 minutes on each side until lightly browned.

2 Combine the herbs, remaining olive oil and balsamic vinegar and mix well. Transfer the eggplant to a serving plate and drizzle over the balsamic mixture. Serve warm or cold.

Grilled Tomatoes with Fresh Oregano and Basil

This recipe accompanies: Barbecued spicy beef (See page 16)

6 ripe tomatoes

⅓ cup olive oil

salt and freshly ground black pepper

¼ cup fresh basil, finely chopped

¼ cup fresh oregano, finely chopped

1 Neatly core the tomatoes and cut in half crosswise. Arrange the halves cut-side up on the barbecue rack or hotplate over medium coals. Brush with oil and sprinkle with salt and black pepper to taste.

2 Cook, turning once or twice, for 3–5 minutes or until heated through. Sprinkle chopped herbs over and serve immediately.

Note: A mixture of mature yellow and red tomatoes will provide attractive colour.

serves 4–8

Foil-Barbecued Potatoes with Herb Butter

This recipe accompanies: Barbequed cheese and onion sausages (See page 19); Pork chops with mango salsa (See page 35)

3½oz/100g butter, softened

¼ cup fresh parsley, chopped

¼ cup fresh thyme, chopped

¼ cup fresh rosemary, chopped

¼ cup fresh basil, chopped

1 teaspoon wholegrain mustard

8 medium baking potatoes

1 Mix together the butter, herbs and mustard until well combined. Roll the mixture up in cling film to form a long log shape and refrigerate until firm.

2 Scrub the potatoes and cook in boiling water for 20 minutes. Drain them and dry well, rub with a little butter or oil and wrap each potato in aluminium foil.

3 Cook the potatoes in coals or on barbecue grill, turning occasionally, for 20 minutes or until tender when pierced with a skewer.

4 To serve, pull back the foil, cut a cross in top of each potato, squeeze open and top with slices of herb butter.

serves 6

Barbecued Corn Cobs

This recipe accompanies: Lamb fillet with mango and mint chutney (See page 28)

4½oz/125g butter, softened

1 small fresh red chilli, finely chopped

¾oz/20g Parmesan cheese, grated

¼ cup fresh coriander, finely chopped

6 corn cobs, husks removed

1 Place the butter, chilli, Parmesan and coriander in a food processor or blender and process until smooth.

2 Light the barbecue. Wrap the corn cobs in a double layer of aluminium foil and cook on barbecue for 30–35 minutes or until corn is tender. To serve, spread corn cobs with chilli butter.

all the extras : sides and snacks • 77

serves 4

Wholegrain Mustard Potatoes

This recipe accompanies: Mustard pork spare ribs (See page 30); Barbecued mustard marinated fish fillets (See page 57)

2lb/1kg new potatoes
¼ cup sour cream
¼ cup mayonnaise
2 tablespoons wholegrain mustard
2 tablespoons olive oil
1 tablespoon lemon juice

1 Cook the potatoes in a large saucepan of boiling water until just tender. Rub off the skins and set the potatoes aside to cool.

2 Mix the sour cream, mayonnaise, mustard, oil and lemon juice in a small bowl. Spoon the mixture over the potatoes. Serve at room temperature.

serves 8

Grilled Garlic Bread

This recipe accompanies: Rosemary lamb skewers (See page 29)

1 long baguette
2 cloves garlic, crushed
¼ teaspoon salt
¼ cup mixed fresh herbs, chopped
4½oz/125g butter, softened

1 Cut the bread into 1in/2½cm slices. Crush the garlic with the salt, then combine thoroughly with the herbs and softened butter.

2 Spread the butter and garlic mixture on both sides of the slices of bread. Grill over medium coals, turning frequently, for approximately 2 minutes or until golden brown.

serves 4

Barbecued Potato Skins

*This recipe accompanies: Lamb burger with grilled haloumi
(See page 24); Tuna with wasabi and sweet soy (See page 58)*

6 large potatoes, scrubbed
olive oil

1 Bake the potatoes in the oven for 1 hour or until
tender. Remove from the oven and set aside until
cool enough to handle. Cut the potatoes in half and
scoop out the flesh, leaving a ¼in/5mm-thick shell
– keep the potato flesh for another use. Cut potato
skins into large pieces and brush with oil.

2 Light the barbecue. Cook the potato skins on the
barbecue for 5–8 minutes each side or until crisp
and golden.

*These potato skins are delicious served with a dip of your
choice.*

*Notes: The reserved potato flesh can be used to make a
potato salad or potato curry, as a topping on a cottage pie,
or to make croquettes.*

makes 20

Barbecued Mushrooms with Chilli Butter

*This recipe accompanies: Mediterranean barbecued chicken
(See page 40); Charcoal grilled prawns (See page 50)*

20 button mushrooms, stalks removed

CHILLI BUTTER
2oz/60g butter, softened
½ fresh red chilli, finely chopped
½ teaspoon ground cumin
¼ cup fresh parsley, finely chopped

1 To make the chilli butter, place the butter, chilli, cumin
and parsley in a food processor or blender and
process until smooth. Wrap the butter in cling film to
form a log shape, then chill until required.

2 Light the barbecue. Cut the butter log into
20 pieces. Place a piece of butter on each
mushroom and cook on barbecue for 4–5 minutes,
or until butter melts and mushrooms are cooked.
Serve immediately with toothpicks.

*These delicious bite-size morsels will disappear as fast as
you can cook them!*

Bacon-Roasted Potatoes

This recipe accompanies: Mixed grill (See page 21);
Yakitori chicken skewers (See page 38)

4 large potatoes, quartered

¼ cup oil

1 tablespoon sesame oil

2 teaspoons salt

6 rindless bacon rashers, finely chopped

¼ teaspoon white pepper

¼ teaspoon grated nutmeg

1 Pre-heat the oven to medium high. Bring a large saucepan of water to the boil. Add the potatoes and cook for 5 minutes, then drain well.

2 Transfer the potatoes to a roasting tin. Drizzle the oils over the top and toss to coat, then sprinkle with salt.

3 Roast the potatoes for 30 minutes, turning occasionally. Sprinkle the bacon, pepper and nutmeg over potatoes and cook for 10 minutes more or until bacon is crisp.

Honey-Baked Carrots

This recipe accompanies: Zesty marinated pork cutlets (See page 33)

2 oz/60 g butter

2 cloves garlic, crushed

2 tablespoons lemon juice

2 tablespoons honey

8 carrots, halved lengthwise

1 Preheat oven to 180°C. Melt the butter in a medium saucepan over gentle heat. Add the garlic and cook for 1 minute. Stir in the lemon juice and honey and mix well.

2 Arrange the carrots in a baking dish. Brush with the honey mixture and bake for 25 minutes, basting frequently.

Spicy Barbecued Beer Nuts

This recipe accompanies: Barbecued thai style steaks (See page 15);
Chicken pesto burger (See page 37)

21oz/600g unhusked peanuts, roasted and salted

1 tablespoon sweet paprika

1 tablespoon ground cumin

2 teaspoons garam masala

1 teaspoon ground coriander

1 teaspoon ground nutmeg

¼ teaspoon cayenne pepper

1 tablespoon olive oil

1   Light the barbecue. Place the peanuts in a bowl. Add the paprika, cumin, garam masala, coriander, nutmeg and cayenne pepper and toss to coat.

2   Heat the oil on the barbecue hotplate, add the nut mixture and cook, turning frequently, for 5 minutes or until the nuts are golden. Cool slightly before serving.

Note: If you do not have a hotplate, cook these inside with a frying pan and bring them out to the barbecue.

The nuts are very hot when first removed from the barbecue, and they retain their heat for quite a long time, so caution your guests when you serve these delicious nibbles.

Warm Marinated Olives

This recipe accompanies: Marinated beef strips (See page 10);
Barbecued chicken burger with aioli (See page 41);
Barbecued noodles (See page 63)

10½oz/300g black olives in brine

10½oz/300g green olives in brine

1 cup extra virgin olive oil

4 bay leaves

4 sprigs rosemary

1 fresh red chilli, sliced

2 cloves garlic, crushed

¼ cup balsamic vinegar

1   Preheat the oven to medium. Drain and rinse the olives and pat dry. Combine all the other ingredients in a deep baking tray and heat until fragrant. Add the olives, stir to combine and cook gently until heated through. Serve warm or cold.

Avocado Salsa

*This recipe goes well with Barbecued cheese and onion sausages
(See page 19); Marinated swordfish steaks (See page 49);
Spring vegetable fritters (See page 66)*

- 2 avocados, cut into ½in/1cm cubes
- 1 tomato, cut into ½in/1cm cubes
- 1 red pepper, cut into ½in/1cm cubes
- 1 cucumber, cut into ½in/1cm cubes
- 8 black olives

DRESSING

- 1 tablespoon honey
- 3 tablespoons cider vinegar
- 5 tablespoons olive oil
- salt and freshly ground black pepper

1 Mix the vegetables and olives in a salad bowl.

2 To make the dressing, whisk the honey, vinegar, oil, salt and pepper together. Drizzle a little dressing over the salad and serve the rest separately.

Sweet Chilli Sauce

*This recipe goes well with Spicy beef burger (See page 20); Sticky lamb ribs
(See page 25); Lamb fillet with mint and mango chutney
(See page 28); Sesame prawn cakes (See page 47); Barbecued noodles
(See page 63); Vege burgers with sweet chilli sauce (See page 61)*

- 150g fresh red chillies, finely sliced
- 2oz/60g fresh ginger, finely sliced
- 4 cloves garlic, finely sliced
- 2 cups cider vinegar
- 700g white sugar
- 1 teaspoon salt

1 Reserve a third of the finely sliced chilli and purée the rest with the ginger, garlic and enough of the vinegar to make a paste. Put the paste and reserved chilli into a saucepan.

2 Add the sugar, salt and the rest of the vinegar. Bring to the boil, lower the heat and simmer until the mixture is syrupy (about 30 minutes).

3 Pour into glass bottles or jars and use as required.

Smoky Eggplant Dip

*This recipe goes well with Moroccan lamb skewers (See page 26); Tuna with wasabi and
sweet soy (See page 58); Barbecued noodles (See page 63)*

- 1 large eggplant
- 2 cloves garlic, unpeeled
- 3oz/85g pitted black olives
- 2–3 teaspoons olive oil
- salt and freshly ground black pepper

1 Cook the whole eggplant on the barbecue for 40 minutes or until soft. Cut in half lengthwise and allow to cool.

2 Scoop the eggplant pulp into a food processor or blender, add the garlic, olives and 2 teaspoons of oil. Purée until smooth, adding the remaining oil if necessary, then season. Serve with raw vegetables and fresh pitta bread for dipping.

Home-made Tomato Sauce

This recipe goes well with Classic beef burger (See page 9);
Vegetarian sausages (See page 62); Vegetable kebabs with home made
tomato sauce (See page 65)

2 tablespoons olive oil

1 large onion, chopped

1 clove garlic, crushed

400g canned chopped tomatoes

2 teaspoons brown sugar

½ cup dry white wine

¼ cup fresh basil, chopped

freshly ground black pepper

1 Heat the oil in a saucepan, add the onion and garlic and cook for 4–5 minutes until softened. Stir in the tomatoes, sugar and wine and simmer for 5 minutes. Add half the basil and simmer for 1 hour or until the sauce is thick.

2 Just before serving, stir in the remaining basil and pepper to taste. Serve with seafood, chicken, steaks or sausages.

serves 4

Spicy Dark Plum Dipping Sauce

This recipe goes well with Chinese barbecued spare ribs (See page 34)

½ cup plum sauce

½ cup soy sauce

¼ cup red wine vinegar

1 clove garlic, crushed

1½ in/4cm piece fresh ginger, grated

3 tablespoons sesame seeds

1 Combine the plum sauce, soy sauce, vinegar, garlic and ginger in a glass bowl. Cover and refrigerate until required. Add sesame seeds just before using.

serves 4

Best Ever Peanut Satay Sauce

This recipe goes well with Beef kebabs (variation 2. See page 18)

1 small onion, finely chopped

1 clove garlic, finely chopped

1 teaspoon dried shrimp paste

¼ teaspoon chilli powder

salt

1 tablespoon peanut oil

⅔ cup crunchy peanut butter

1 tablespoon tamarind paste

1 teaspoon brown sugar

1 Place the onion, garlic and shrimp paste in a blender or food processor and process to make a smooth paste. Add the chilli powder and salt and briefly process to mix well.

2 Heat the peanut oil in a saucepan over a medium heat, add the spice paste and fry gently, stirring, for a few seconds. Add 1¼ cups of water and bring to the boil, then add the peanut butter, tamarind paste and sugar and mix to combine. Simmer, stirring frequently, until the sauce thickens. Pour into a bowl and serve warm with assorted satays.

Notes: This sauce can be made well ahead and reheated gently, and is delicious with chicken, beef, lamb or seafood satays.

Sweet-and-Sour Barbecue Sauce

This recipe goes well with Bacon and chorizo sausage kebabs (See page 36)

1 tablespoon vegetable oil
1 small onion, chopped
1 red pepper, chopped
1 tablespoon soy sauce
2 tablespoons honey
1 tablespoon tomato paste
2 tablespoons cornflour
½ cup cider vinegar
½ cup chicken stock
440g canned pineapple pieces, drained

1 Heat the oil in a saucepan and cook the onion and pepper for 4–5 minutes or until soft. In a bowl, mix together the soy sauce, honey, tomato paste, cornflour and vinegar.

2 Stir the cornflour mixture into the vegetables, then stir in the stock. Cook over a medium heat for 2–3 minutes, stirring frequently, until the sauce boils and thickens. Stir in the pineapple pieces and cook for 2–3 minutes longer.

Note: A sweet-and-sour sauce is always a popular accompaniment for chicken and pork, but is also delicious served with sausages and fish.

Quick Tangy Barbecue Sauce

This recipe goes well with Classic steak and onion sandwiches (See page 11); Veal schnitzel burger (See page 13); Bacon beef and cheese burger (See page 17)

2oz/60g butter
1 small onion, chopped
¼ cup red wine vinegar
2 tablespoons brown sugar
2 teaspoons Dijon mustard
½ teaspoon salt
1 teaspoon freshly ground black pepper
¼ teaspoon paprika
1 thick slice of lemon
1 cup tomato sauce
1 tablespoon Worcestershire sauce
1 teaspoon soy sauce

1 Melt the butter in a saucepan. Add the onion and cook for 2–3 minutes. Stir in the vinegar, sugar, mustard, salt, pepper, paprika and ½ cup water. Add the lemon slice and simmer for 30 minutes, stirring occasionally.

2 Remove the lemon, stir in the remaining ingredients and cook for 15 minutes more. Use as a basting sauce or an accompaniment.

‹ Chilli Plum Marinade and Grilling Sauce

½ cup hoisin sauce
¼ cup plum sauce
¼ cup soy sauce
¼ cup dry white wine
2 tablespoons sugar
3 cloves garlic, crushed
1 fresh red chilli, sliced
1 teaspoon sesame oil

This recipe goes well with Scallops with plum glaze (see page 48)

1 Place all the ingredients in a medium bowl and mix well to combine.

2 Use to marinate your choice of meat or seafood for at least 30 minutes before cooking. Also use for basting during cooking.

desserts

The Finishing Touch

serves 4

Pancakes with Strawberries and Ice Cream

9oz/250g strawberries, hulled and halved

2 tablespoons strawberry liqueur

⅓ cup caster sugar, plus 2 tablespoons

1½ cups self-raising flour

finely grated zest of 1 lemon

2 eggs, separated

1½ cups milk

1oz/30g butter, melted

1 Toss the strawberries, liqueur and 2 tablespoons caster sugar together in a bowl and set aside.

2 Place the flour, caster sugar and the lemon zest in a bowl. Add the egg yolks, milk and butter and mix to combine. Place the egg whites in a separate bowl and beat until soft peaks form, then fold into the batter.

3 Heat and lightly oil a frying pan. Cook spoonfuls of the mixture for 2–3 minutes on each side or until golden and cooked through. Keep warm until all the pancakes are cooked.

4 Top the pancakes with the strawberries and serve with ice cream.

❯

VARIATIONS

- Fold 4½oz/125g blueberries through the batter before cooking and serve as above.

- For banana pancakes, make the pancakes as above but instead of the strawberries, slice 3 peeled bananas and cook in a frying pan with 2 tablespoons of butter and 3 tablespoons of brown sugar until caramelised and golden. Serve on the pancakes with ice cream.

serves 6

Barbecued Bananas with Cinnamon

6 large, slightly green bananas
2oz/60g butter, melted
1 tablespoon freshly squeezed lime juice
2 tablespoons brown sugar
½ teaspoon cinnamon
1 tablespoon rum

1 Cut the unpeeled bananas in half lengthwise. Brush the cut sides with melted butter, then sear, cut-side down, on barbecue grill over hot coals.

2 Turn the bananas over and move them to a cooler part of the grill. Sprinkle with the lime juice, sugar, cinnamon and rum and cook until the skins have blackened and the flesh is soft. Serve in the skins.

VARIATIONS

• Use fresh peach halves instead of bananas and cook until tender, not blackened.

• Use 1in/2½ cm-thick slices of peeled pineapple instead of the bananas and substitute Malibu for the rum. Cook until tender and golden. Serve sprinkled with toasted, shredded coconut.

serves 6

Grilled Pineapple

finely grated zest of ½ lemon
1 tablespoon brown sugar
½oz/15g butter, melted
1 small ripe pineapple

1 Light the barbecue and oil the grill bars. Combine the lemon zest, brown sugar and melted butter.

2 Peel the pineapple, then cut into rings and remove the core. Place on the barbecue and cook for 1 minute each side, then brush with the sugar mixture and cook for 2 minutes each side. Serve with ice cream.

>

VARIATIONS
• Use halved stone fruit, such as plums, peaches or mango with the skin on, instead of the pineapple.

serves 6–8

Strawberry and Apple Tart

23cm pre-cooked sweet pastry flan case
400ml thick custard

STRAWBERRY FILLING
1oz/30g butter
3 cooking apples, cored, peeled and diced
2 teaspoons lemon juice
1lb/500g small strawberries, hulled
2 tablespoons caster sugar
1 teaspoon nutmeg

1 To make the filling, melt the butter in a frying pan and cook the apples with lemon juice over a high heat for 2–3 minutes or until tender. Remove from the heat and add the strawberries. Set aside and allow to cool completely, then stir in the sugar and nutmeg.

2 Spoon the custard into pastry case, top with strawberry filling. Serve with cream or ice cream.

> VARIATIONS
• Instead of the apples, use 3 stoned, diced peaches or other stone fruit, such as apricots or plums. If you prefer, you can use a mixture of different berries instead of only strawberries.

serves 6

Barbecued Tropical Fruit Salad Skewers

½ cup grated palm sugar

½ teaspoon ground cinnamon

½ teaspoon ground nutmeg

¼ cup white rum

2 teaspoons vanilla extract

½ fresh melon, cut into 1in/2½cm cubes

½ fresh pineapple, cut into 1in/2½cm cubes

2 ripe yellow bananas, peeled, each cut into 6 pieces

9oz/250g fresh strawberries, hulled

2 kiwifruit, peeled and cut into 6 pieces

¼ cup toasted coconut

1 Mix the palm sugar and spices in a small bowl. Stir in the rum and vanilla until the sugar is dissolved. Alternately thread the fruit onto skewers, then brush with the spice mixture and allow to stand for 5 minutes.

2 Barbecue for 10 minutes or until lightly browned, turning occasionally and basting with the spice mixture. Serve sprinkled with toasted coconut.

> VARIATIONS
- Make a chocolate sauce with 5½oz/150g dark chocolate melted with ¼ cup cream. Serve with the skewers for dipping.

Barbequed Pears

13oz/375g firm ricotta

¼ cup double cream

¼ cup nut-flavoured liqueur (optional)

½ cup fresh mint, chopped

1oz/30g butter, melted

2 tablespoons brown sugar

6 dessert pears, halved and cored

12 walnut halves, roughly chopped

6 sprigs mint

1 In a bowl, combine the cheese, cream and liqueur (if using). Add the chopped mint and beat until smooth, then refrigerate.

2 Mix the melted butter and sugar together and brush over pears. Place a sheet of baking paper on the grill bars of the barbecue and pierce several times with a sharp knife – this is to stop the sugar from overheating too quickly and burning. Place the pears on the baking paper and grill on both sides until tender.

3 Top each pear with a few tablespoons of the cheese mixture, sprinkle with the walnuts, garnish with mint sprigs and serve.

Note: The pears for this dessert should be perfectly ripe but still relatively firm — avoid any bruised fruit.

>

VARIATIONS

- Replace the ricotta with mascarpone, and add ¼ cup dried cranberries to the cheese mixture. Sprinkle with chopped macadamias instead of walnuts.

- This recipe also works well with halved, cored apples or halved, stoned peaches.

Apple Tarts

1 sheet ready-rolled puff pastry, thawed

1 egg yolk

2 Granny Smith apples, peeled, cored and very finely sliced

1 tablespoon clear honey

1 tablespoon caster sugar

1   Preheat the oven to 190°C. Line an oven tray with baking paper. Cut the pastry sheet into 4 squares, then cut a ¼in/5mm strip from each side of each square. Brush the squares with egg yolk, then place the pastry strips around the edges of each square to form a lip.

2   Brush each pastry case with egg yolk again, place on the prepared trays and bake for 10 minutes.

3   Arrange the apple slices in the centre of each pastry case, brush with honey and sprinkle with sugar. Bake for a further 15 minutes, then serve immediately with whipped cream.

> VARIATIONS

- Use peeled, cored and finely sliced pears instead of apples.

- Add 6 hulled and sliced strawberries to the tarts with the apples.

Rhubarb and Strawberries with Cream

4 stalks rhubarb

9oz/250g fresh strawberries, hulled

¼ cup sugar

1 Preheat the oven to 190°C. Wash and trim the rhubarb, then cut into 1in/2½cm pieces. Place in an 8in/21cm oval oven dish. Add the strawberries and sprinkle with sugar.

2 Bake for 20 minutes until rhubarb is tender and juices are bubbling. Serve with double cream and extra fresh strawberries.

VARIATIONS

- Try this recipe with peeled, cored and diced apple instead of the strawberries, or with 5 diced fresh peaches instead of the rhubarb.

Baked apples with Walnuts

6 small, red, crisp apples

½ cup fresh white breadcrumbs

½ cup chopped walnuts

¼ cup brown sugar

zest of 1 orange

1 tablespoon sultanas

2oz/60g butter, melted

1 Remove the core from the apples with a small, pointed knife. Cut out a little more apple flesh to widen the hole. Chop the flesh finely and add to the breadcrumbs, then mix in the walnuts, sugar, orange zest, sultanas and half the melted butter.

2 Pack the stuffing into the apples and place them on the barbecue using indirect heat or elevate on the wire rack over direct heat. Cook for 30 minutes. Serve with cream or ice cream.

VARIATIONS

- Replace the walnuts with almonds and the sultanas with diced, dried apricots.

- Try this stuffing in halved, stoned peaches with coconut instead of the finely chopped apple flesh.

serves 4

Lemon and Sugar Crêpes

1 cup plain flour
1 cup milk
2 tablespoons caster sugar
2 eggs
1oz/30g butter, melted

1 Place the flour, milk, caster sugar, eggs and melted butter into a blender. Blend on medium speed until well mixed. Pour through a strainer into a jug, then allow to rest for 1 hour.

2 Place an oiled non-stick crêpe pan over medium heat. Add enough crêpe mixture to just cover the bottom of the pan when you tilt it – if there is too much in the pan, pour it back into the jug. Cook for about 1 minute until golden, then flip and cook second side until golden. Remove from the pan to a warm plate and cover with foil while you continue cooking the rest.

3 Serve warm with lemon wedges and sugar.

❯

- - - VARIATIONS - - -

• When the crêpes are cooked, place a few slices of banana on each one and sprinkle with some brown sugar. Roll the crêpe up with the banana inside and put on a grill plate over low heat until the banana softens and cooks. Serve with ice cream.

• Hull and quarter 9oz/250g strawberries. Mix in a bowl with 2 tablespoons sugar and 2 tablespoons strawberry liqueur. Place a tablespoon of this mixture on each crêpe and fold into quarters. Serve with extra strawberries and cream.

index